To His Coy Mistress

ANDREW MARVELL

A Phoenix Paperback

This edition published in 1996 by Phoenix,
a Division of Orion Books Ltd,
Orion House, 5 Upper St Martin's Lane, London WC2H 9EA

Cover illustration: Portrait of Diana Kirke, by Sir Peter Lely,
Yale Center for British Art, Paul Mellon Collection

ISBN 1 85799 669 0

Typeset by CentraCet Ltd, Cambridge
Printed in Great Britain by
Clays Ltd, St Ives plc

Contents

To his Coy Mistress

Had we but World enough, and Time
This coyness Lady were no crime.
We would sit down, and think which way
To walk, and pass our long Loves Day.
Thou by the *Indian Ganges* side
Should'st Rubies find: I by the Tide
Of *Humber* would complain. I would
Love you ten years before the Flood:
And you should if you please refuse
Till the Conversion of the *Jews*.
My vegetable Love should grow
Vaster then Empires, and more slow.
An hundred years should go to praise
Thine Eyes, and on thy Forehead Gaze.
Two hundred to adore each Breast:
But thirty thousand to the rest.
An Age at least to every part,
And the last Age should show your Heart.
For Lady you deserve this State;
Nor would I love at lower rate.
   But at my back I alwaies hear
Times winged Charriot hurrying near:
And yonder all before us lye

Desarts of vast Eternity.
Thy Beauty shall no more be found,
Nor, in thy marble Vault, shall sound
My ecchoing Song: then Worms shall try
That long preserv'd Virginity:
And your quaint Honour turn to dust;
And into ashes all my Lust.
The Grave's a fine and private place,
But none I think do there embrace.

Now therefore, while the youthful hew
Sits on thy skin like morning dew,
And while thy willing Soul transpires
At every pore with instant Fires,
Now let us sport us while we may;
And now, like am'rous birds of prey,
Rather at once our Time devour,
Than languish in his slow-chapt pow'r.
Let us roll all our Strength, and all
Our sweetness up into one Ball:
And tear our Pleasures with rough strife,
Thorough the Iron gates of Life.
Thus, though we cannot make our Sun
Stand still, yet we will make him run.

The Coronet

When for the Thorns with which I long, too
   long,
   With many a piercing wound,
   My Saviours head have crown'd,
I seek with Garlands to redress that Wrong:
   Through every Garden, every Mead,
I gather flow'rs (my fruits are only flow'rs)
   Dismantling all the fragrant Towers
That once adorned my Shepherdesses head.
And now when I have summ'd up all my store,
   Thinking (so I my self deceive)
   So rich a Chaplet thence to weave
As never yet the king of Glory wore:
   Alas I find the Serpent old
   That, twining in his speckled breast,
   About the flow'rs disguis'd does fold,
   With wreaths of Fame and Interest.
Ah, foolish Man, that would'st debase with them
And mortal Glory, Heaven's Diadem!
But thou who only could'st the Serpent tame,
Either his slipp'ry knots at once untie,
And disintangle all his winding Snare:
Or shatter too with him my curious frame:
And let these wither, so that he may die,
Though set with Skill and chosen out with Care. 3

That they, while Thou on both their Spoils dost tread,
May crown thy Feet, that could not crown thy Head,

Bermudas

Where the remote *Bermudas* ride
In th' Oceans bosome unespy'd,
From a small Boat, that row'd along,
The listning Winds receiv'd this Song.
     What should we do but sing his Praise
That led us through the watry Maze,
Unto an Isle so long unknown,
And yet far kinder than our own?
Where he the huge Sea-Monsters wracks,
That lift the Deep upon their Backs.
He lands us on a grassy Stage;
Safe from the Storms, and Prelat's rage,
He gave us this eternal Spring,
Which here enamells every thing;
And sends the Fowl's to us in care,
On daily Visits through the Air.
He hangs in shades the Orange bright,
Like golden Lamps in a green Night.
And does in the Pomgranates close,
Jewels more rich than *Ormus* show's.
He makes the Figs our mouths to meet;
And throws the Melons at our feet.

But Apples plants of such a price,
No Tree could ever bear them twice.
With Cedars, chosen by his hand,
From *Lebanon*, he stores the Land.
And makes the hollow Seas, that roar,
Proclaime the Ambergris on shoar.
He cast (of which we rather boast)
The Gospels Pearl upon our Coast.
And in these Rocks for us did frame
A Temple, where to sound his Name.
Oh let our Voice his Praise exalt,
Till it arrive at Heavens Vault:
Which thence (perhaps) rebounding, may
Eccho beyond the *Mexique Bay*.
Thus sung they, in the *English* boat,
An holy and a chearful Note,
And all the way, to guide their Chime,
With falling Oars they kept the time.

The Nymph complaining for the death of her Faun

The wanton Troopers riding by
Have shot my Faun and it will dye.
Ungentle men! They cannot thrive
To kill thee. Thou neer didst alive
Them any harm: alas nor could

5

Thy death yet do them any good.
I'me sure I never wisht them ill;
Nor do I for all this; nor will:
But, if my simple Pray'rs may yet
Prevail with Heaven to forget
Thy murder, I will Joyn my Tears
Rather then fail. But, O my fears!
It cannot dye so. Heavens King
Keeps register of every thing:
And nothing may we use in vain.
Ev'n Beasts must be with Justice slain;
Else Men are made their *Deodands*.
Though they should wash their guilty hands
In this warm life blood, which doth part
From thine, and wound me to the Heart,
Yet could they not be clean: their Stain
Is dy'd in such a Purple Grain.
There is not such another in
The World, to offer for their Sin.

Unconstant *Sylvio*, when yet
I had not found him counterfeit,
One morning (I remember well)
Ty'd in this silver Chain and Bell,
Gave it to me: nay and I know
What he said then; I'me sure I do.
Said He, look how your Huntsman here
Hath taught a Faun to hunt his *Dear*.
But *Sylvio* soon had me beguil'd.

This waxed tame; while he grew wild,
And quite regardless of my Smart,
Left me his Faun, but took his Heart.

   Thenceforth I set my self to play
My solitary time away,
With this: and very well content,
Could so mine idle Life have spent
For it was full of sport; and light
Of foot, and heart; and did invite,
Me to its game: it seem'd to bless
Its self in me. How could I less
Than love it? O I cannot be
Unkind, t' a Beast that loveth me.

   Had it liv'd long, I do not know
Whether it too might have done so
As *Sylvio* did: his Gifts might be
Perhaps as false or more than he.
But I am sure, for ought that I
Could in so short a time espie,
Thy Love was far more better then
The love of false and cruel men.

   With sweetest milk, and sugar, first
I it at mine own fingers nurst.
And as it grew, so every day
It wax'd more white and sweet than they.
It had so sweet a Breath! And oft
I blusht to see its foot more soft,
And white, (shall I say then my hand?)

NAY any Ladies of the Land.

It is a wond'rous thing, how fleet
'Twas on those little silver feet.
With what a pretty skipping grace,
It oft would challenge me the Race:
And when 'thad left me far away,
'Twould stay, and run again, and stay.
For it was nimbler much than Hindes;
And trod, as on the four Winds.

I have a Garden of my own,
But so with Roses over grown,
And Lillies, that you would it guess
To be a little Wilderness.
And all the Spring time of the year
It onely loved to be there.
Among the beds of Lillyes, I
Have sought it oft, where it should lye;
Yet could not, till it self would rise,
Find it, although before mine Eyes.
For, in the flaxen Lillies shade,
It like a bank of Lillies laid.
Upon the Roses it would feed,
Until its Lips ev'n seem'd to bleed:
And then to me 'twould boldly trip,
And print those Roses on my Lip.
But all its chief delight was still
On Roses thus its self to fill:
And its pure virgin Limbs to fold

In whitest sheets of Lillies cold.
Had it liv'd long, it would have been
Lillies without, Roses within.

    O help! O help! I see it faint:
And dye as calmely as a Saint.
See how it weeps. The Tears do come
Sad, slowly dropping like a Gumme.
So weeps the wounded Balsome: so
The holy Frankincense doth flow.
The brotherless *Heliades*
Melt in such Amber Tears as these.

    I in a golden Vial will
Keep these two crystal Tears; and fill
It till it do o'reflow with mine;
Then place it in *Diana's* Shrine.

    Now my sweet Faun is vanish'd to
Whether the Swans and Turtles go:
In fair *Elizium* to endure,
With milk-white Lambs, and Ermins pure
O do not run too fast: for I
Will but bespeak they Grave, and dye.

    First my unhappy Statue shall
Be cut in Marble; and withal,
Let it be weeping too: but there
Th' Engraver sure his Art may spare;
For I so truly thee bemoane,
That I shall weep though I be Stone:
Until my Tears, still dropping, wear

My breast, themselves engraving there.
There at my feet shalt thou be laid,
Of purest Alabaster made:
For I would have thine Image be
White as I can, though not as Thee.

Young Love

1

Come little Infant, Love me now,
    While thine unsuspected years
Clear thine aged Fathers brow
    From cold Jealousie and Fears.

2

Pretty surely 'twere to see
    By young Love old Time beguil'd:
While our Sportings are as free
    As the Nurses with the Child.

3

Common beauties stay fifteen;
    Such as yours should swifter move;
Whose fair Blossoms are too green
    Yet for Lust, but not for Love.

4

Love as much the snowy Lamb
   Or the wanton Kid does prize,
As the lusty Bull or Ram,
   For his morning Sacrifice.

5

Now then love me: time may take
   Thee before thy time away:
Of this Need wee'l Virtue make,
   And learn Love before we may.

6

So we win of doubtful Fate;
   And, if good she to us meant,
We that Good shall antedate,
   Or, if ill, that Ill prevent.

7

Thus as Kingdomes, frustrating
   Other Titles to their Crown,
In the craddle crown their King,
   So all Forraign Claims to drown,

8

So, to make all Rivals vain,
   Now I crown thee with my Love:

Crown me with thy Love again,
    And we both shall Monarchs prove.

The Picture of little T. C. in a Prospect of Flowers

1

See with what simplicity
This Nimph begins her golden daies!
In the green Grass she loves to lie,
And there with her fair Aspect tames
The Wilder flow'rs, and gives them names:
But only with the Roses playes;
            And them does tell
What Colour best becomes them, and what Smell.

2

Who can foretel for what high cause
This Darling of the Gods was born!
Yet this is She whose chaster Laws
The wanton Love shall one day fear,
And, under her command severe.
See his Bow broke and Ensigns torn.
            Happy, who can
Appease this virtuous Enemy of Man!

3

O then let me in time compound,
And parly with those conquering Eyes;
Ere they have try'd their force to wound,
Ere, with their glancing wheels, they drive
In Triumph over Hearts that strive,
And them that yield but more despise.
            Let me be laid,
Where I may see thy Glories from some Shade.

4

Mean time, whilst every verdant thing
It self does at thy Beauty charm,
Reform the errours of the Spring;
Make that the Tulips may have share
Of sweetness, seeing they are fair;
And Roses of their thorns disarm;
               But most procure
That Violets may a longer Age endure.

5

But O young beauty of the Woods,
Whom Nature courts with fruits and flow'rs,
Gather the Flow'rs, but spare the Buds;
Lest *Flora* angry at thy crime,
To kill her Infants in their prime,
Do quickly make th' Example Yours;

And, ere we see,
Nip in the blossome all our hopes and Thee.

The Garden

1

How vainly men themselves amaze
To win the Palm, the Oke, or Bayes;
And their uncessant Labours see
Crown'd from some single Herb or Tree,
Whose short and narrow verged Shade
Does prudently their Toyles upbraid;
While all Flow'rs and all Trees do close
To weave the Garlands of repose.

2

Fair quiet, have I found thee here,
And Innocence thy Sister dear!
Mistaken long, I sought you then
In busie Companies of Men.
Your sacred Plants, if here below,
Only among the Plants will grow.
Society is all but rude,
To this delicious Solitude.

3

No white nor red was ever seen
So am'rous as this lovely green.
Fond Lovers, cruel as their Flame,
Cut in these Trees their Mistress name.
Little, Alas, they know, or heed,
How far these Beauties Hers exceed!
Fair Trees! where s'eer your barkes I wound,
No Name shall but your own be found.

4

When we have run our Passions heat,
Love hither makes his best retreat.
The *Gods*, that mortal Beauty chase.
Still in a Tree did end their race.
Apollo hunted *Daphne* so,
Only that She might Laurel grow.
And *Pan* did after *Syrinx* speed,
Not as a Nymph, but for a Reed.

5

What wond'rous Life in this I lead!
Ripe Apples drop about my head;
The Luscious Clusters of the Vine
Upon my Mouth do crush their Wine;
The Nectaren, and curious Peach,
Into my hands themselves do reach;

Stumbling on Melons, as I pass,
Insnar'd with Flow'rs, I fall on Grass.

6

Mean while the Mind, from pleasure less,
Withdraws into its happiness:
The Mind, that Ocean where each kind
Does streight its own resemblance find;
Yet it creates, transcending these,
Far other Worlds, and other Seas;
Annihilating all that's made
To a green Thought in a green Shade.

7

Here at the Fountains sliding foot,
Or at some Fruit-trees mossy root,
Casting the Bodies Vest aside,
My Soul into the boughs does glide:
There like a Bird it sits, and sings,
Then whets, and combs its silver Wings;
And, till prepar'd for longer flight,
Waves in its Plumes the various Light.

8

Such was that happy Garden-state,
While Man there walk'd without a Mate:
After a Place so pure, and sweet,
What other Help could yet be meet!

But 'twas beyond a Mortal's share
To wander solitary there:
Two Paradises 'twere in one
To live in Paradise alone.

9

How well the skilful Gardner drew
Of flow'rs and herbes this Dial new;
Where from above the milder Sun
Does through a fragrant Zodiack run;
And, as it works, th' industrious Bee
Computes its time as well as we.
How could such sweet and wholsome Hours
Be reckon'd but with herbs and flow'rs!

Upon Appleton House, to my Lord Fairfax

1

Within this sober Frame expect
Work of no Forrain *Architect*;
That unto Caves the Quarries drew,
And Forrests did to Pastures hew;
Who of his great Design in pain
Did for a Model vault his Brain,
Whose Columnes should so high be rais'd
To arch the Brows that on them gaz'd.

2

Why should of all things Man unrul'd
Such unproportion'd dwellings build?
The Beasts are by their Denns exprest:
And Birds contrive an equal Nest;
The low roof'd Tortoises do dwell
In cases fit of Tortoise-shell:
No Creature loves an empty space;
Their Bodies measure out their Place.

3

But He, superfluously spread,
Demands more room alive then dead.
And in his hollow Palace goes
Where Winds as he themselves may lose.
What need of all this Marble Crust
T'impark the wanton Mote of Dust,
That thinks by Breadth the World t'unite
Though the first Builders fail'd in Height?

4

But all things are composed here
Like Nature, orderly and near:
Be which we the Dimensions find
Of that more sober Age and Mind,
When larger sized Men did stoop
To enter at a narrow loop;

As practising, in doors so strait,
To strain themselves through *Heavens Gate*.

5

And surely when the after Age
Shall hither come in *Pilgrimage*,
These sacred Places to adore,
By *Vere* and *Fairfax* trod before,
Men will dispute how their Extent
Within such dwarfish Confines went:
And some will smile at this, as well
As *Romulus* his Bee-like Cell.

6

Humility alone designs
Those short but admirable Lines,
By which, ungirt and unconstrain'd,
Things greater are in less contain'd.
Let others vainly strive t'immure
The *Circle* in the *Quadrature*!
These *holy Mathematicks* can
In ev'ry Figure equal Man.

7

Yet thus the laden House does sweat,
And scarce indures the *Master* great:
But where he comes the swelling Hall
Stirs, and the *Square* grows *Spherical*;

More by his *Magnitude* distrest,
Then he is by its straitness prest:
And too officiously it slights
That in it self which him delights.

8

So Honour better Lowness bears,
Then That unwonted Greatness wears.
Height with a certain Grace does bend,
But low Things clownishly ascend.
And yet what needs there here Excuse,
Where ev'ry Thing does answer Use?
Where neatness nothing can condemn,
Nor Pride invent what to contemn?

9

A Stately *Frontispice of Poor*
Adorns without the open Door:
Nor less the Rooms within commends
Daily new *Furniture of Friends*.
The House was built upon the Place
Only as for a *Mark of Grace*;
And for an *Inn* to entertain
Its *Lord a while, but not remain*.

10

Him *Bishops-Hill*, or *Denton* may,
Or *Bilbrough*, better hold then they:

But Nature here hath been so free
As if she said leave this to me.
Art would more neatly have defac'd
What she had laid so sweetly wast;
In fragrant Gardens, shady Woods,
Deep Meadows, and transparent Floods.

11

While with slow Eyes we these survey,
And on each pleasant footstep stay,
We opportunly may relate
The Progress of this Houses Fate.
A *Nunnery* first gave it birth.
For *Virgin Buildings* oft brought forth.
And all that Neighbour-Ruine shows
The Quarries whence this dwelling rose.

12

Near to this gloomy Cloysters Gates
There dwelt the blooming Virgin *Thwates*;
Fair beyond Measure, and an Heir
Which might Deformity make fair.
And oft She spent the Summer Suns
Discoursing with the *Suttle Nunns*.
Whence in those Words one to her weav'd,
(As 'twere by Chance) Thoughts long conceiv'd.

13

'Within this holy leisure we
'Live innocently as you see.
'These Walls restrain the World without,
'But hedge our Liberty about.
'These Bars inclose that wider Den
'Of those wild Creatures, called Men.
'The Cloyster outward shuts its Gates,
'And, from us, locks on them the Grates.

14

'Here we, in shining Armour white,
'Like *Virgin Amazons* do fight.
'And our chast *Lamps* we hourly trim,
'Lest the great *Bridegroom* find them dim.
'Our *Orient* Breaths perfumed are
'With insense of incessant Pray'r.
'And Holy-water of our Tears
'Most strangly our Complexion clears.

15

'Not Tears of Grief; but such as those
'With which calm Pleasure overflows;
'Or Pity, when we look on you
'That live without this happy Vow.
'How should we grieve that must be seen
'Each one a *Spouse* and each a *Queen*;

'And can in *Heaven* hence behold
'Our brighter Robes and Crowns of Gold?

16

'When we have prayed all our Beads,
'Some One the holy *Legend* reads;
'While all the rest with Needles paint
'The Face and Graces of the *Saint*.
'But what the Linnen can't receive
'They in their Lives do interweave.
'This Work the *Saints* best represents;
'That serves for *Altar s Ornaments*.

17

'But much it to our work would add
'If here your hand, your Face we had:
'By it we would *our Lady* touch;
'Yet thus She you resembles much.
'Some of your Features, as we sow'd,
'Through ev'ry *Shrine* should be bestow'd.
'And in one Beauty we would take
'Enough a thousand *Saints* to make.

18

'And (for I dare not quench the Fire
'That me does for your good inspire)
''Twere Sacriledge a Man t'admit
'To holy things, for *Heaven* fit.

'I see the *Angels* in a Crown
'On you the Lillies show'ring down:
'And round about you Glory breaks,
'That something more then humane speaks,

19

'All Beauty, when at such a height,
'Is so already consecrate.
'*Fairfax* I know; and long ere this
'Have mark'd the Youth, and what he is.
'But can he such a *Rival* seem
'For whom you *Heav'n* should disesteem?
'Ah, no! and 'twould more honour prove
'He your *Devoto* were, then *Love*.

20

'Here live beloved, and obey'd:
'Each one your Sister, each your Maid.
'And, if our Rule seem strictly pend,
'The Rule it self to you shall bend.
'Our *Abbess* too, now far in Age,
'Doth your succession near presage.
'How soft the yoke on us would lye,
'Might such fair Hands as yours it tye!

21

'Your voice, the sweetest of the Quire,
'Shall draw *Heav'n* nearer, raise us higher.

'And your Example, if our Head,
'Will soon us to perfection lead.
'Those Virtues to us all so dear,
'Will straight grow Sanctity when here:
'And that, once sprung, increase so fast
'Till Miracles it work at last.

22

'Nor is our *Order* yet so nice,
'Delight to banish as a Vice.
'Here Pleasure Piety doth meet:
'One perfecting the other Sweet.
'So through the mortal fruit we boyl
'The Sugars uncorrupting Oyl:
'And that which perisht while we pull,
'Is thus preserved clear and full.

23

'For such indeed are all our Arts;
'Still handling Natures finest Parts.
'Flow'rs dress the Altars; for the Clothes,
'The Sea-born Amber we compose;
'Balms for the griv'd we draw; and Pasts
'We mold, as Baits for curious tasts.
'What need is here of Man? unless
'These as sweet Sins we should confess.

24

'Each Night among us to your side
'Appoint a fresh and Virgin Bride;
'Whom if *our Lord* at midnight find,
'Yet Neither should be left behind.
'Where you may lye as chast in Bed,
'As Pearls together billeted.
'All Night embracing Arm in Arm,
'Like Chrystal pure with Cotton warm.

25

'But what is this to all the store
'Of Joys you see, and may make more!
'Try but a while, if you be wise:
'The Tryal neither Costs, nor Tyes.'
Now *Fairfax* seek her promis'd faith:
Religion that dispensed hath;
Which She hence forward does begin;
The *Nuns* smooth Tongue has suckt her in.

26

Oft, though he knew it was in vain,
Yet would he valiantly complain.
'Is this that *Sanctity* so great,
'An Art by which you finly'r cheat?
'Hypocrite Witches, hence *avant*
'Who though in prison yet inchant!

'Death only can such Theeves make fast,
'As rob though in the Dungeon cast.

27

'Were there but, when this House was made,
'One Stone that a just Hand had laid,
'It must have fall'n upon her Head
'Who first Thee from thy Faith misled.
'And yet, how well soever ment,
'With them 'twould soon grow fraudulent:
'For like themselves they alter all,
'And vice infects the very Wall.

28

'But sure those Buildings last not long,
'Founded by Folly, kept by Wrong.
'I know what Fruit their Gardens yield,
'When they it think by Night conceal'd.
'Fly from their Vices. 'Tis thy state,
'Not Thee, that they would consecrate.
'Fly from their Ruine. How I fear
'Though guiltless lest thou perish there.'

29

What should he do? He would respect
Religion, but not Right neglect:
For first Religion taught him Right,
And dazled not but clear'd his sight.

Sometimes resolv'd his Sword he draws,
But reverenceth then the Laws:
For Justice still that Courage led;
First from a Judge, then Souldier bred.

30

Small Honour would be in the Storm.
The *Court* him grants the lawful Form;
Which licens'd either Peace or Force,
To hinder the unjust Divorce.
Yet still the *Nuns* his Right debar'd,
Standing upon their holy Guard.
Ill-counsell'd Women, do you know
Whom you resist, or what you do?

31

Is not this he whose Offspring fierce
Shall fight through all the *Universe*;
And with successive Valour try
France, Poland, either *Germany*;
Till one, as long since prophecy'd,
His Horse through conquer'd *Britain* ride?
Yet, against Fate, his Spouse they kept;
And the great Race would intercept.

32

Some to the Breach against their Foes
Their *Wooden Saints* in vain oppose.

Another bolder stands at push
With their old *Holy-Water Brush*.
While the disjointed *Abbess* threads
The gingling Chain-shot of her *Beads*.
But their lowd'st Cannon were their Lungs;
And sharpest Weapons were their
    Tongues.

33
But, waving these aside like Flyes,
Young *Fairfax* through the Wall does rise,
Then th' unfrequented Vault appear'd,
And superstitions vainly fear'd.
The *Relicks false* were set to view;
Only the Jewels there were true.
But truly bright and holy *Thwaites*
That weeping at the *Altar* waites.

34
But the glad Youth away her bears,
And to the *Nuns* bequeaths her Tears:
Who guiltily their Prize bemoan,
Like Gipsies that a Child hath stoln.
Thenceforth (as when th' Inchantment
    ends
The Castle vanishes or rends)
The wasting Cloister with the rest
Was in one instant dispossest.

At the demolishing, this Seat
To *Fairfax* fell as by Escheat.
And what both *Nuns* and *Founders* will'd
'Tis likely better thus fulfill'd.
For if the *Virgin* prov'd not theirs,
The *Cloyster* yet remained hers.
Though many a *Nun* there made her Vow,
'Twas no *Religious House* till now.

From that blest Bed the *Heroe* came,
Whom *France* and *Poland* yet does fame:
Who, when retired here to Peace,
His warlike Studies could not cease;
But laid these Gardens out in sport
In the just Figure of a Fort;
And with five Bastions it did fence,
As aiming one for ev'ry Sense.

When in the *East* the Morning Ray
Hangs out the Colours of the Day,
The Bee through these known Allies hums,
Beating the *Dian* with its *Drumms*.
Then Flow'rs their drowsy Eylids raise,
Their Silken Ensigns each displayes,

And dries its Pan yet dank with Dew,
And fills its Flask with Odours new.

38

These, as their *Governour* goes by,
In fragrant Vollyes they let fly;
And to salute their *Governess*
Again as great a charge they press:
None for the *Virgin Nymph*; for She
Seems with the Flow'rs a Flow'r to be.
And think so still! though not compare
With Breath so sweet, or Cheek so faire.

39

Well shot ye Firemen! Oh how sweet,
And round your equal Fires do meet;
Whose shrill report no Ear can tell,
But Ecchoes to the Eye and smell.
See how the Flow'rs, as at *Parade*,
Under their *Colours* stand displaid:
Each *Regiment* in order grows,
That of the Tulip Pinke and Rose.

40

But when the vigilant *Patroul*
Of Stars walks round about the *Pole*,
Their Leaves, that to the stalks are curl'd,
Seem to their Staves the *Ensigns* furl'd.

Then in some Flow'rs beloved Hut
Each Bee as Sentinel is shut;
And sleeps so too but, if once stir'd,
She runs you through, nor askes *the Word*.

41

Oh Thou, that dear and happy Isle
The Garden of the World ere while,
Thou *Paradise* of four Seas,
Which *Heaven* planted us to please,
But, to exclude the World, did guard
With watry if not flaming Sword;
What luckless Apple did we tast,
To make us Mortal, and The Wast?

42

Unhappy! shall we never more
That sweet *Militia* restore,
When Gardens only had their Towrs,
And all the Garrisons were Flowrs,
When Roses only Arms might bear,
And Men did rosie Garlands wear?
Tulips, in several Colours barr'd,
Were then the *Switzers* of our *Guard*.

43

The *Gardiner* had the *Souldiers* place,
And his more gentle Forts did trace.

The Nursery of all things green
Was then the only *Magazeen*.
The *Winter Quarters* were the Stoves,
Where he the tender Plants removes.
But War all this doth overgrow:
We Ord'nance Plant and Powder sow.

44

And yet there walks one on the Sod
Who, had it pleased him and *God*,
Might once have made our Gardens spring
Fresh as his own and flourishing.
But he preferr'd to the *Cinque Ports*
These five imaginary Forts:
And, in those half-dry Trenches, spann'd
Pow'r which the Ocean might command.

45

For he did, with his utmost Skill,
Ambition weed, but *Conscience* till.
Conscience that Heaven-nursed Plant,
Which most our Earthly Gardens want.
A prickling leaf it bears, and such
As that which shrinks at ev'ry touch;
But Flowrs eternal, and divine,
That in the Crowns of Saints do shine.

46

The sight does from these *Bastions* ply,
Th' invisible *Artilery*;
And at proud *Cawood Castle* seems
To point the *Battery* of its Beams.
As if it quarrell'd in the Seat
Th' Ambition of its *Prelate* great.
But ore the Meads below it plays,
Or innocently seems to gaze.

47

And now to the Abbyss I pass
Of that unfathomable Grass,
Where Men like Grashoppers appear,
But Grashoppers are Gyants there:
They, in their squeking Laugh, contemn
Us as we walk more low then them:
And, from the Precipices tall
Of the green spir's, to us do call.

48

To see Men through this Meadow
    Dive,
We wonder how they rise alive.
As, under Water, none does know
Whether he fall through it or go.
But, as the Marriners that sound,
And show upon their Lead the Ground,

They bring up Flow'rs so to be seen,
And prove they've at the Bottom been.

49

No Scene that turns with Engines strange
Does oftner then these Meadows change.
For when the Sun the Grass hath vext,
The tawny Mowers enter next;
Who seem like *Israelites* to be,
Walking on foot through a green Sea.
To them the Grassy Deeps divide,
And crowd a Lane to either Side.

50

With whistling Sithe, and Elbow strong,
These Massacre the Grass along:
While one, unknowing, carves the *Rail*,
Whose yet unfeather'd Quils her fail.
The Edge all bloody from its Breast
He draws, and does his stroke detest;
Fearing the Flesh untimely mow'd
To him a Fate as black forebode.

51

But bloody *Thestylis*, that waites
To bring the mowing Camp their Cates.
Greedy as Kites has trust it up,
And forthwith means on it to sup:

When on another quick She lights,
And cryes, he call'd us *Israelites*;
But now, to make his saying true,
Rails rain for Quails, for Manna Dew.

52

Unhappy Birds! what does it boot
To build below the Grasses Root;
When Lowness is unsafe as Hight,
And Chance o'retakes what scapeth spight?
And now your Orphan Parents Call
Sounds your untimely Funeral.
Death-Trumpets creak In such a Note,
And 'tis the *Sourdine* in their Throat.

53

Or sooner hatch or higher build:
The Mower now commands the Field;
In whose new Traverse seemeth wrought
A Camp of Battail newly fought:
Where, as the Meads with Hay, the Plain
Lyes quilted ore with Bodies slain:
The Women that with forks it fling,
Do represent the Pillaging.

54

And now the careless Victors play,
Dancing the Triumphs of the Hay;

Where every Mowers wholesome Heat
Smells like an *Alexanders sweat*.
Their Females fragrant as the Mead
Which they in *Fairy Circles* tread:
When at their Dances End they kiss,
Their new-made Hay not sweeter is.

55

When after this 'tis pil'd in Cocks,
Like a calm Sea it shews the Rocks:
We wondring in the River near
How Boats among them safely steer.
Or, like the *Desert Memphis Sand*,
Short *Pyramids* of Hay do stand.
And such the *Roman Camps* do rise
In Hills for Soldiers Obsequies.

56

This *Scene* again withdrawing brings
A new and empty Face of things;
A levell'd space, as smooth and plain,
As Clothes for *Lilly* strecht to stain.
The World when first created sure
Was such a Table rash and pure.
Or rather such is the *Toril*
Ere the Bulls enter at Madril.

57

For to this naked equal Flat,
Which *Levellers* take Pattern at,
The Villagers in common chase
Their Cattle, which it closer rase;
And what below the Sith increast
Is pincht yet nearer by the Beast.
Such, in the painted World, appear'd
Davenant with th' Universal Heard.

58

They seem within the polisht Grass
A Landskip drawen in Looking-Glass
And shrunk in the huge Pasture show
As Spots, so shap'd, on Faces do.
Such Fleas, ere they approach the Eye,
In Multiplying Glasses lye.
They feed so wide, so slowly move,
As *Constellations* do above.

59

Then, to conclude these pleasant
    Acts,
Denton sets ope its *Cataracts*;
And makes the Meadow truly be
(What it but seem'd before) a Sea.
For, jealous of its *Lords* long stay,
It try's t'invite him thus away.

The River in it self is drown'd,
And Isl's th' astonish'd Cattle round.

60

Let others tell the *Paradox*,
How Eels now bellow in the Ox;
How Horses at their Tails do kick,
Turn'd as they hang to Leeches quick;
How Boats can over Bridges sail;
And Fishes do the Stables scale.
How *Salmons* trespassing are found;
And Pikes are taken in the Pound.

61

But I, retiring from the Flood,
Take Sanctuary in the Wood;
And, while it lasts, my self imbark
In this yet green, yet growing Ark;
Where the first Carpenter might best
Fit Timber for his Keel have Prest.
And where all Creatures might have shares;
Although in Armies, not in Paires.

62

The double Wood of ancient Stocks
Link'd in so thick, an Union locks,
It like two *Pedigrees* appears,
On one hand *Fairfax*, th' other *Veres*:

Of whom though many fell in War,
Yet more to Heaven shooting are:
And, as they Natures Cradle deckt;
Will in green Age her Hearse expect.

63

When first the Eye this Forrest sees
It seems indeed as *Wood* not *Trees*:
As if their Neighbourhood so old
To one great Trunk them all did mold.
There the huge Bulk takes place, as ment
To thrust up a *Fifth Element*;
And stretches still so closely wedg'd
As if the Night within were hedg'd.

64

Dark all without it knits; within
It opens passable and thin;
And in as loose an order grows,
As the *Corinthean Porticoes*.
The arching Boughs unite between
The Columnes of the Temple green;
And underneath the winged Quires
Echo about their tuned Fires.

65

The *Nightingale* does here make choice
To sing the Tryals of her Voice.

Low Shrubs she sits in, and adorns
With Musick high the squatted Thorns.
But highest Oakes stoop down to hear,
And listning Elders prick the Ear.
The Thorn, lest it should hurt her, draws
Within the Skin its shrunken claws.

66

But I have for my Musick found
A Sadder, yet more pleasing Sound:
The *Stock-doves*, whose fair necks are grac'd
With Nuptial Rings their Ensigns chast;
Yet always, for some Cause unknown,
Sad pair unto the Elms they moan.
O why should such a Couple mourn,
That in so equal Flames do burn!

67

Then as I careless on the Bed
Of gelid *Straw-berryes* do tread,
And through the Hazles thick espy
The hatching *Thrastles* shining Eye;
The *Heron* from the Ashes top,
The eldest of its young lets drop,
As if it Stork-like did pretend
That *Tribute* to *its Lord* to send.

68

But most the *Hewel's* wonders are,
Who here has the *Holt-feisters* care.
He walks still upright from the Root,
Meas'ring the Timber with his Foot;
And all the way, to keep it clean,
Doth from the Bark the Wood-moths glean.
He, with his Beak, examines well
Which fit to stand and which to fell.

69

The good he numbers up, and hacks;
As if he mark'd them with the Ax.
But where he, tinkling with his Beak,
Does find the hollow Oak to speak,
That for his building he designs,
And through the tainted Side he mines.
Who could have thought the *tallest Oak*
Should fall by such a *feeble Strok'*!

70

Nor would it, had the Tree not fed
A *Traitor-worm*, within it bred.
(As first our *Flesh* corrupt within
Tempts impotent and bashful *Sin*.)
And yet that *Worm* triumphs not long,
But serves to feed the *Hewels young*.

While the Oake seems to fall content,
Viewing the Treason's Punishment.

71

Thus I, *easie Philosopher*,
Among the *Birds* and *Trees* confer:
And little now to make me, wants
Or of the *Fowles, or of the Plants*.
Give me but Wings as they, and I
Streight floting on the Air shall fly:
Or turn me but, and you shall see
I was but an inverted Tree.

72

Already I begin to call
In their most learned Original:
And where I Language want, my Signs
The Bird upon the Bough divines;
And more attentive there doth sit
Then if She were with Lime-twigs knit.
No Leaf does tremble in the Wind
Which I returning cannot find.

73

Out of these scattr'd *Sibyls* Leaves
Strange *Prophecies* my Phancy weaves:
And in one History consumes,
Like *Mexique Paintings*, all the *Plumes*.

What *Rome*, *Greece*, *Palestine*, ere said
I in this light *Mosaick* read.
Thrice happy he who, not mistook,
Hath read in *Natures mystick Book*.

74

And see how Chance's better Wit
Could with a Mask my studies hit!
The Oak-Leaves me embroyder all,
Between which Caterpillars crawl:
And Ivy, with familiar trails,
Me licks, and clasps, and curles, and hales.
Under this *antick Cope* I move
Like some great *Prelate of the Grove*,

75

Then, languishing with ease, I toss
On Pallets swoln of Velvet Moss;
While the Wind, cooling through the Boughs,
Flatters with Air my panting Brows.
Thanks for my Rest ye *Mossy Banks*,
And unto you *cool Zephyr's* Thanks,
Who, as my Hair, my Thoughts too shed,
And winnow from the Chaff my head.

76

How safe, methinks, and strong, behind
These Trees have I incamp'd my Mind;

Where Beauty, aiming at the Heart,
Bends in some Tree its useless Dart;
And where the World no certain Shot
Can make, or me it toucheth not.
But I on it securely play,
And gaul its Horsemen all the Day.

77

Bind me ye *Woodbines* in your 'twines,
Curle me about ye gadding *Vines*,
And Oh so close your Circles lace,
That I may never leave this Place:
But, lest your Fetters prove too weak,
Ere I your Silken Bondage break,
Do you, *O Brambles*, chain me too,
And courteous *Briars* nail me through.

78

Here in the Morning tye my Chain,
Where the two Woods have made a Lane:
While, like a *Guard* on either side,
The Trees before their *Lord* divide;
This, like a long and equal Thread,
Betwixt two *Labyrinths* does lead.
But, where the Floods did lately drown,
There at the Ev'ning stake me down.

For now the Waves are fal'n and dry'd,
And now the Meadows fresher dy'd;
Whose Grass, with moister colour dasht,
Seems as green Silks but newly washt.
No *Serpent* new nor *Crocodile*
Remains behind our little *Nile*;
Unless it self you will mistake,
Among these Meads the only Snake.

See in what wanton harmless folds
It ev'ry where the Meadow holds;
And its yet muddy back doth lick,
Till as a *Chrystal Mirrour* slick;
Where all things gaze themselves, and doubt
If they be in it or without.
And for his shade which therein shines,
Narcissus like, the *Sun* too pines.

Oh what a Pleasure 'tis to hedge
My Temples here with heavy sedge;
Abandoning my lazy Side,
Stretcht as a Bank unto the Tide;
Or to suspend my sliding Foot
On the Osiers undermined Root,

And in its Branches tough to hang,
While at my Lines the Fishes twang!

82

But now away my Hooks, my Quills,
And Angles, idle Utensils.
The *young Maria* walks to night:
Hide trifling Youth thy Pleasures slight.
'Twere shame that such judicious Eyes
Should with such Toyes a Man surprize;
She that already is the *Law*
Of all her *Sex*, her *Ages Aw*.

83

See how loose Nature, in respect
To her, it self doth recollect;
And every thing so whisht and fine,
Starts forth with to its *Bonne Mine*.
The *Sun* himself, of *Her* aware
Seems to descend with greater Care:
And lest *She* see him go to Bed,
In blushing Clouds conceales his Head.

84

So when the Shadows laid asleep
From underneath these Banks do creep,
And on the River as it flows
With *Eben Shuts* begin to close;

The modest *Halcyon* comes in sight,
Flying betwixt the Day and Night;
And such an horror calm and dumb,
Admiring Nature does benum.

85

The viscous Air, wheres'ere She fly,
Follows and sucks her Azure dy;
The gellying Stream compacts below,
If it might fix her shadow so;
The stupid Fishes hang, as plain
As *Flies in Chrystal* overt'ane;
And Men the silent *Scene* assist,
Charm'd with the *Saphir-winged Mist*.

86

Maria such, and so doth hush
The *World*, and through the *Ev'ning* rush.
No new-born *Comet* such a Train
Draws through the Skie, nor Star new-slain.
For streight those giddy Rockets fail,
Which from the putrid Earth exhale,
But by her *Flames*, in *Heaven* try'd,
Nature is wholly *vitrifi'd*.

87

'Tis *She* that to these Gardens gave
That wondrous Beauty which they have;

She streightness on the Woods bestows;
To *Her* the Meadow sweetness owes;
Nothing could make the River be
So Chrystal-pure but only *She*;
She yet more Pure, Sweet, Streight, and Fair,
Then Gardens, Woods, Meads, Rivers are.

88

Therefore what first *She* on them spent,
They gratefully again present.
The Meadow Carpets where to tread;
The Garden Flow'rs to Crown *Her* head;
And for a Glass the limpid Brook,
Where *She* may all *her* Beautyes look;
But, since *She* would not have them seen,
The Wood about *her* draws a Skreen.

89

For *She*, to higher Beauties rais'd,
Disdains to be for lesser prais'd.
She counts her Beauty to converse
In all the Languages as *hers*;
Nor yet in those *her* self imployes
But for the *Wisedome*, not the *Noyse*;
Nor yet that *Wisdome* would affect,
But as 'tis *Heavens Dialect*.

Blest Nymph! that couldst so soon prevent
Those *Trains* by Youth against thee meant;
Tears (watry Shot that pierce the Mind;)
And *Sighs* (Loves Cannon charg'd with Wind;)
True Praise (That breaks through all defence;)
And *feign'd complying Innocence*;
But knowing where this *Ambush* lay,
She scap'd the sage, but roughest Way.

This 'tis to have been from the first
In a *Domestick Heaven* nurst,
Under the *Discipline severe*
Of *Fairfax* and the starry *Vere*;
Where not one object can come nigh
But pure, and spotless as the Eye;
And *Goodness* doth it self intail
On *Females*, if there want a *Male*.

Go now fond Sex that on your Face
Do all your useless Study place,
Nor once at Vice your Brows dare knit
Lest the smooth Forehead wrinkled sit:
Yet your own Face shall at you grin,
Thorough the Black-bag of your Skin;

When *knowledge* only could have fill'd
And *Virtue* all those *Furrows* till'd.

93

Hence *She* with Graces more divine
Supplies beyond her *Sex* the *Line*;
And, like a *sprig* of *Misleto*
On the *Fairfacian* Oak does grow;
Whence, for some universal good,
The *Priest* shall cut the sacred Bud;
While her *glad Parents* most rejoice,
And make their *Destiny* their *Choice*.

94

Mean time ye Fields, Springs, Bushes, Flow'rs,
Where yet She leads her studious Hours,
(Till Fate her worthily translates,
And find a *Fairfax* for our *Thwaites*)
Employ the means you have by Her,
And in your kind your selves preferr;
That, as all *Virgins* She preceds,
So you all *Woods, Streams, Gardens, Meads*.

95

For you *Thessalian Tempe's Seat*
Shall now be scorn'd as obsolete;
Aranjuez, as less, disdain'd;
The *Bel-Retiro* as constrain'd;

But name not the *Idalian Grove*,
For 'twas the Seat of wanton Love;
Much less the Dead's *Elysian Fields*,
Yet nor to them your Beauty yields.

96

'Tis not, what once it was, the *World*:
But a rude heap together hurl'd;
All negligently overthrown,
Gulfes, Deserts, Precipices, Stone.
Your lesser *World* contains the same.
But in more decent Order tame;
*You Heaven's center, Nature's Lap.
And Paradice's* ony *Map.*

97

But now the *Salmon-Fisher's* moist
Their *Leathern Boats* begin to hoist;
And, like *Antipodes* in Shoes,
Have shod their *Heads* in their *Canoos.*
How *Tortoise* like, but not so slow,
These rational *Amphibii* go?
Let's in: for the dark *Hemisphere*
Does now like one of them appear.

An Horatian Ode upon Cromwel's Return from Ireland

The forward Youth that would appear
Must now forsake his *Muses* dear,
    Nor in the Shadows sing
    His Numbers languishing
'Tis time to leave the Books in dust,
And oyl th'unused Armours rust,
    Removing from the Wall
    The Corslet of the Hall.
So restless *Cromwel* could not cease
In the inglorious Arts of Peace,
    But through adventrous War
    Urged his active Star.
And, like the three fork'd Lightning, first
Breaking the Clouds where it was nurst,
    Did thorough his own Side
    His fiery way divide.
For 'tis all one to Courage high
The Emulous or Enemy;
      And with such to inclose
      Is more then to oppose.
Then burning through the Air he went,
And Pallaces and Temples rent:
      And *Cæsar*s head at last
      Did through his Laurels blast.

'Tis Madness to resist or blame
The force of angry Heavens flame:
    And, if we would speak true,
    Much to the Man is due.
Who, from his private Gardens, where
He liv'd reserved and austere,
    As if his highest plot
    To plant the Bergamot,
Could by industrious Valour climbe
To ruine the great Work of Time,
    And cast the Kingdome old
    Into another Mold.
Though Justice against Fate complain,
And plead the antient Rights in vain:
    But those do hold or break
    As Men are strong or weak.
Nature that hateth emptiness,
Allows of penetration less:
    And therefore must make room
    Where greater Spirits come.
What Field of all the Civil Wars,
Where his were not the deepest Scars?
    And *Hampton* shows what part
    He had Of wiser Art.
Where, twining subtile fears with hope,
He wove a Net of such a scope,
    That *Charles* himself might chase
    To *Caresbrooks* narrow case.

That thence the *Royal Actor* born
The *Tragick Scaffold* might adorn:
    While round the armed Bands
    Did clap their bloody hands.
He nothing common did or mean
Upon that memorable Scene:
    But with his keener Eye
    The Axes edge did try:
Nor call'd the *Gods* with vulgar spight
To vindicate his helpless Right,
    But bow'd his comely Head,
    Down as upon a Bed.
This was that memorable Hour
Which first assur'd the forced Pow'r.
    So when they did design
    The *Capitols* first Line,
A bleeding Head where they begun,
Did fright the Architects to run;
    And yet in that the *State*
    Foresaw it's happy Fate.
And now the *Irish* are asham'd
To see themselves in one Year tam'd
    So much one Man can do,
    That does both act and know.
They can affirm his Praises best,
And have, though overcome, confest
    How good he is, how just,
    And fit for highest Trust:

Nor yet grown stiffer with Command,
But still in the *Republick's* hand:
    How fit he is to sway
    That can so well obey.
He to the *Commons Feet* presents
A *Kingdome*, for his first years rents:
    And, what he may, forbears
    His Fame to make it theirs:
And has his Sword and Spoyls ungirt,
To lay them at the *Publick's* skirt.
    So when the Falcon high
    Falls heavy from the Sky,
She, having kill'd, no more does search,
But on the next green Bow to pearch;
    Where, when he first does lure,
    The Falckner has her sure.
What may not then our *Isle* presume
While Victory his Crest does plume!
    What may not others fear
    If thus he crown each Year!
A *Cæsar* he ere long to *Gaul*,
To *Italy* an *Hannibal*,
    And to all States not free
    Shall *Clymacterick* be.
The *Pict* no shelter now shall find
Within his party-colour'd Mind;
    But from this Valour sad
    Shrink underneath the Plad:

Happy if in the tufted brake
The *English Hunter* him mistake;
    Nor lay his Hounds in near
    The *Caledonian* Deer.
But thou the Wars and Fortunes Son
March indefatigably on:
    And for the last effect
    Still keep thy Sword erect;
Besides the force it has to fright
The Spirits of the shady Night,
    The same *Arts* that did *gain*
    A *Pow'r* must it *maintain*.

A Note on Andrew Marvell

Andrew Marvell (1621–78), the English poet, parliamentarian, and satirist, was born at Winestead in Holderness, Yorkshire, where his father was rector. He was educated at Hull Grammar School and Trinity College, Cambridge. At the outbreak of the Civil War his sympathies were not fixed, though he seems to have associated with the Royalists. He travelled abroad and, in the 1650s, was committed to the Parliamentary cause, acting as tutor to the daughter of Lord Fairfax who had recently retired as a Parliamentary general. His two years at Fairfax's Yorkshire seat, Nun Appleton House, probably saw the writing of much of his lyric and philosophical poetry. He then became tutor to a ward of Oliver Cromwell's and, in 1657, assistant Latin secretary to the government. In 1659 he became MP for Hull, the constituency he represented until his death. Whether or not he supported the Restoration, he became reconciled to it and remained a loyal, if independent, critic of the political scene.

Some of his earlier poems ('Fleckno', 'Tom May's
Death', and 'The Character of Holland') had been satiri-

cally motivated, and during the Restoration he turned to writing satirical pamphlets and prose works. The most significant are: *The Rehearsal Transprosed*, 1672 (with a *Second Part*, 1673), in which he advocated religious toleration, and *An Account of the Growth of Popery, and Arbitrary Government*, 1677, which is a scathing review of Charles II's reign.

His reputation in his own day, and in the following century, was as a champion of liberty and toleration, and as a polemicist. Today his reputation stands very high, and rests largely on a remarkably small number of extremely skilful and graceful, but perplexing and intriguing, poems, which were published posthumously, as *Miscellaneous Poems*, in 1681. They include love lyrics, pastorals, and religious poems, executed with a compelling mixture of lyric grace and dialectical urgency and complexity, which links Marvell with both Donne and Jonson. In the extreme wit of a poem like 'The Definition of Love' he seems almost to be a 'Metaphysical Poet', but in the sequence of pastorals on gardens he is reminiscent of the Elizabethan lyricists. Typically, he mixes dialectical argument with sensuous evocation and hints of covert meaning or allegory in a manner which is rich and suggestive, though it is often difficult to determine *precisely* what he means, or what is his attitude to the subject (as, for example, in the marvellously complex 'Nymph complaining for the Death of Her Fawn'). In 'To his Coy Mistress' and 'An Horatian Ode Upon Cromwell's

Return from Ireland' he produced, respectively, the most searching seduction and political poems in the language. Part of his quality lies in a certain irreducible ambiguity, where he attempts to reconcile Platonic ideals with human reality, allegory with the facts of history, and the mysteries of religion with the limitations of morality.